Invis-Abilities

Faith White

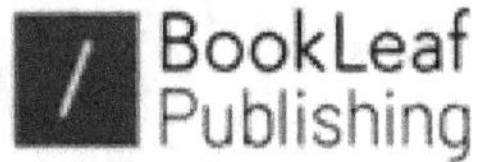

Presentation by *BookLeaf Publishing*

Web: www.bookleafpub.com

E-mail: info@bookleafpub.com

ISBN : 9789357211154

First edition 2022

DEDICATION

Alaska - Be brave, little bird, for who you are is beautiful

Wilder - I love you more than more

Jeff - You are the melody my harmony needs to make a song

PREFACE

The inspiration for these poems came from the social-emotional standards we have been asked to teach our students. While every academic standard presents its own challenges, these principles for living are the most difficult of all. I can confidently teach students skills I know I have mastered. These skills, however, are seemingly impossible superpowers. They don't always work as intended. Some of our triumphs in life are celebrated, but usually it seems like people only notice when we fail. I want my students to know that each attempt they make to be the best human they can be makes them a hero in my eyes.

Casting

I'm the hero of my story
Main character, top billing
That means I am responsible
For plotlines that need filling
I'm the hero of my story
The camera follows me
From my wardrobe to my hairdo
Everything's planned to a T
I'm the hero of my story
Every entrance underscored
My lines have been closed captioned
And I cannot be ignored

I'm the villain of my story
Making mountains out of hills
I refuse to learn my lesson
Make bad choices for the thrills
I'm the villain of my story
Cutting corners in the game
No one's sad when I'm the loser
I'm the biggest one to blame
I'm the villain of my story
Fueled by jealousy and rage
I can hear the people booing
When I step onto the stage

I'm the cranky silly sidekick
I'm the wise guy with a wand
I'm the damsel in distress
I'm the talking frogs in ponds
I'm the ruler, the explorer
I'm the orphan, I'm the king
I'm the person in the background
No one else is noticing
I'm the author of this story
Writing one page at a time
I'm the audience who's watching
Pass the popcorn; this life's mine

My Dog Bones

I face a lot of problems
(Like every human's life)
Except I have a dog who tries
To rescue me from strife
His gadgetry is limited
Can't even use a phone
And so he solves each issue
With miscellaneous bones

When he sees me crying
He digs on my behalf
Soon he's retrieved a funny bone
Admittedly I laugh
A look of longing prompts
A wishbone we can split
He lets me win and keep the wish
He has no need for it

A T(ea) bone when I'm thirsty
Bare bones for when I'm poor
I've worked my fingers to the bone
And feel it in them more
Bones can be quite fragile
Since sticks and stones might break them
On days with complications

He's advised me not to make them

He always knows which bone to pick
Though you might think it crazy
My favorite is when he knows
The bone I want is lazy
More often I require
A strong bone to brace my back
I've learned to use my bone head
Compensate for skills I lack

He doesn't have a jealous bone
Bad-to-the-bone's for fools
The skeletons my closet holds
Are all my greatest tools
My dog's so smart and understands
He shows it with his gifts
That's why I will forgive him
For the places that he sniffs

Smell Your Own Breath

Have you smelled your own breath lately?
Sure, we notice others' breath
What about yours?
Little wafts
And whiffs
Whispers
Of what you've eaten
And whether you've washed
Flowing in and out
Without thinking
Quick breaths
Slow breaths
Each with a bouquet
Do your words have a scent
An aroma left behind
One that lasts longer
Than the sounds they make?

Head in the Clouds

Grown-ups have jobs
It's what they do
Not-growns have upping
To navigate through
When I was told
My job was to grow
I guessed what it meant
How else could I know
I stretched and I strained
And measured each inch
At first I believed
This would be quite a cinch
Babies grow quickly
New clothes every week
My head got much stronger
I started to speak
The taller I got
Perspectives were altered
Those growing pains hurt
But I never faltered
Into my teen years
My peers found their height
I wasn't done yet
It didn't feel right
And so I continued

To swell and expand
No ceiling contained me
I found ways to stand
When I had aged
Till my hair had gone white
The others faced downwards
Like plants without light
Not me, I'd determined
I'd never comply
Why would I choose earth
There's room in the sky
Higher and higher
Far past what's allowed
All my hard work
Brought my head to the clouds
You may hear it said
Clouds aren't made for you
But what do they know
They can't see the view

Where the Time Goes

I sent myself
On a noble quest
To find the answers
Without the test
I thought it could
Provide some rest
Since nobody knows where the time goes

While it's here
We spare it, spend it
Make it, waste it
Kill it, End it
Do we even
Comprehend it
For nobody knows where the time goes

Our memories
Not always shared
In tough times it's not
Measured fair
Looking for
Some more to spare
Yet nobody knows where the time goes

I looked in wrinkles
And baby's eyes
Though it heals wounds
I was surprised
You can't save time
It always flies
So nobody knows where the time goes

I never found
Its hiding place
No storage shed
In outer space
All I learned
Is it's not a race
And nobody knows where the time goes

The Bottom of My Bag

It's been a long time since I've seen
The bottom of my bag
Who knows what I'd find there?
Fingernail clippers
Hidden by zippers
Receipts storing gum
A ring for my thumb
A postcard of John Glenn
A pen, a yen
A five and a ten
A note from a friend
Gift cards I won't spend
Where does it end?
I should probably take a look

It's been a long time since I've seen
The bottom of my bag
Who knows what I'd find there?
My diary key
Dead flies and a bee
A nameless phone number
Earplugs fit for slumber
The tickets required
That gadget I wired
Bet coupons expired

A gauge for your tires
I might have some pliers
Or matches for fires
I should probably take a look

It's been a long time since I've seen
The bottom of my bag
Who knows what I'd find there?
It's tricky
Sticky
Icky
Too dark to view
But if turned inside out…
Yes, that's what I'll do!
Wipe down
And clean up
Till it sparkles like new
This bag deserves
To be properly used
I'll empty the pockets
And keep the essentials
And throw away anything
Inconsequential
I should probably take a look

Wait…
Would I feel better
Knowing just what I'd find?
Would I miss the guessing

What I'd left behind?

It's been a long time since I've seen
The bottom of my bag
Who knows what I'd find there?
If I end the mystery
No longer burying
That might feel wrong
Forgetting the history
The things I'd been carrying
All along

Black-Eyed Susan

Do you know Black-Eyed Susan?
Black-Eyed Susan knows herself
Don't you dare call her Daisy

I bet you'll find her in the sun
She craves it
Lives for it
Lives through it
Without it
She's unreliable
Unlikely to show her colors
With it
She shines

When grounded
And fed
She'll withstand the toughest conditions
Can't knock her down
She reaches higher
Spreads wider
Taking over
Intimidating the others
Until only she remains

I wonder if her confidence gets lonely

She does love to surprise you
Showing up
In unexpected places
With her brightness
And her hair
Have you noticed her hair?
She'll tickle your nose, dear
Stay away

Still she's not immune
To disease
Even the water she drinks
The water she holds out in front of her
Can make her sick
Be careful, Susan
Don't be sluggish, Susan

When she's given all she can
She rests
Resets
Listens to the birdsongs
Allows herself to be carried
She'll be strong again soon
Then you can find her
Black-Eyed Susan
Both same and new
Dancing with the butterflies
Wild

The Stood Tree

In the forest
In the wood
May not notice
One called "Stood"
It wouldn't ask
It wouldn't shout
It bears no fruit
It does not sprout
It simply stands
And waits for you
It won't branch out
It's stumped, it's true
In fact it never
Thinks to tell
You what it wants
It's just as well
I doubt that it
Could name its need
Stood doesn't know
The way to feed
If you pass by
It may not grieve
The expectation's
That you'll leave

Can Stood be helped
The others wonder
Stood waits for you
To stop and stand under

Without

You can't hatch an egg without breaking the
shell
You can't mend a tear without glue
You can't hear a song without quiet around
You can't shop at stores without shoes
You can't share a smile without letting teeth
show
You can try, but you'll only find frowns
You can't drink a full glass of water, my friend,
Without first turning it upside down

The Spotlight

WANTED: One light
Including installation
Must be available immediately
High quality
Long lasting
With adjustable dimmers
Will need to be able
To shine on and highlight
Without blinding

Actually…
Make that two lights
One to lighten the road ahead
One to showcase what's behind

Perhaps two more
To shine on those next to us
Left and right

A light
To share
Everyone deserves a turn
In the spotlight

Silent Letters

If you want
Your words heard better
Don't ignore
The silent letters
Doesn't mean
You need to yell
The subtleties
Must each be spelled
Without aggression
Elemental
That your speech
Is firm and gentle
To those who don't
Know how to whisper
I've developed
Quite a list for
You to use
To set things straight
Effectively
Communicate
You modulate
You change your tone
You make adjustments
On your own
When you recite

Intended scripts
Each sound deserves
Time on your lips
The tongue - it flicks
It taps and oohs
If you should mumble
Shame on you
If you must talk
A mouth is not
The only thing
To share your thought
Your ears, I'd say,
Play bigger roles
To monitor
The stories told
Not only what is said
But why
And how; for that
You'll need your eyes
Now, blind men will not
Disbelieve
He'll see the message
Get received
By using every
Sense he has
Each breath and movement
Heard, whereas,
In fact, it seems
A whole head's needed

For otherwise
You must concede it
Fails to transfer
Won't be clear
Can't blame for what
They didn't hear
And if they don't
Hear your tree fall
It's like it never
Fell at all

Zookeeper

What can the zookeeper
Bring a flamingo?
Tiny crustaceans
Are their kind of lingo.

What does the zookeeper
Do as chimps grow?
Measure and track,
Keep their records just so.

What can the zookeeper
Do for the bear?
Clean his enclosure
And sweep up loose hair.

How can the zookeeper
Help a sick sloth?
Serve it some medicine
(Not chicken broth.)

What if the zookeeper
Can't help the mice?
They call the vet,
Trusting experts' advice.

What does the zookeeper
Need from the zoo?
Those who are helpful
Need help from you, too.

Food for Thought

I won't sugarcoat
The way the cookie crumbles
Baking is messy

Bad egg, bad apple
You fool me with your roundness
Rotten to the core

A couch potato
Is not for you to sit on
Tiny, starchy rock

I wish I could be
The greatest thing since sliced bread
Like toast or bagels

"Bring home the bacon,"
My mother instructed me.
Time for a playdate?

Spilt milk made them cry
There may be even more tears
When you spill the beans

A cucumber's not

Very cool in a garden
When it's hot outside

The top banana
Has a lovely view for now
(Can't reach, so it rots)

Each option seemed good
Both apples and oranges
Except the lemon

A hard nut to crack
Taken with a grain of salt
Is still quite nutty

Two peas in a pod
Were pleasant until planted
Right in a pickle

It's a piece of cake
That's what I thought. But, in fact,
I ate humble pie.

What Pants Shall I Wear Today

My trousers match my jacket
My sparkly pants are fun
Not every pants
Can handle dance
I need the perfect ones

My culottes let my legs breathe
My buttoned pants are tight
It's hard to sit
And they might split
Now that would be a sight

My belt is a necessity
For jeans worn every day
If they're too loose
Then my caboose
Will be put on display

My bell bottoms look groovy
My sweatpants work for sleep
I have no clue
What jodhpurs do
Don't really need to keep

My linen pants need ironing
My shorts-not-pants suit summer
And for sport
Could wear a skort
Though that might be a bummer

My cargo pants have pockets
My overalls for chores
Stirrups, cropped
I have to opt
To cover up my drawers

I'm really very lucky
I have many pants to pick
When all is told
I'm getting cold
I'd better choose some quick

Life Doesn't Have

Life doesn't have
A lost and found
Where you can find
Your name
And claim
The things you didn't
Care for.
Therefore
If there's doubt
The only route
Is keep looking
Or go without.

Life doesn't have
A narrator
Who will describe
Explain
What's plain
You're only seeing
Your side.
Course I'd
Rather see
All POVs
And so my truth's not
Guaranteed.

Life doesn't have
An outline sketched
To color within.
With labels
You're able
To follow the guide.
I think
With ink
It is scary
So I'm wary.
Are permanent choices
Necessary?

Fire Hydrant

Install a fire hydrant
For next time there's a flame
You'll need supply of water
And hose with which to aim

Always wear your seatbelt
To keep you in your place
Bumps will never warn you
Rarely have the time to brace

Pack a full first aid kit
If you cannot bring a nurse
Injuries are painful
But with no gauze - it's worse

Disaster may not happen
Still we wear our parachute
And put a hole inside it
Since we know that air flows through

Do something today
To make tomorrow better
Though we can't see the future
Fires are easier when wetter

The Special

Order the special
Trust me
The chef who named it so
Knows the menu
Then you
Wear your Sunday best
What makes you feel special
What makes you feel proud
The special may be gone
Might not last
Could run out
Besides
If you save yourself
(The best parts of yourself)
For a rainy day
In a zany way
You might forget
That
You
Are
Great
Don't have to wait
Eat on good plates
With your best mates
After all

You deserve special

Monsters

I'm on a monster hunt
I'm checking under beds
Investigating who stars in
The nightmares in their heads

While on my monster hunt
I found a varied crew
A closer look revealed to me
That monsters have fears, too

The yeti is ashamed
Those big feet make them cry
Their signature appendage
Is a thing they'd rather hide

The cyclops also struggles
Self-confidence is tough
You see one eye atop their face
And think that's not enough

The bogeyman or woman
Resents its rank and role
You're repulsed with horror
Won't appreciate the whole

The goblin's angst is boredom
It shudders to repeat
The absence of abnormal
Leads its spirit to deplete

The ogre fights their anger
Don't tell them what to do
Your rules and regulations
Fuel their raging point of view

The zombie works alone
So it'd rather not compete
If you seem a threat then there
May not be much to eat

The vampire's veiled from daytime
Fears what they can't observe
And what if only darkness is
The life that they deserve

Fears are quite diverse
They range in size and shape
The unifying element
Is needing to escape

Before you go to sleep
Beneath your bed is shown
Reminders that although we're scared
At least we're not alone

On This Bench Rests

On this bench rests
A tiny tot
She needs a nap
Or maybe not
She holds the gift
Her grandma bought
I hope their day is blessed

On this bench rests
A "cheerful" child
Hair and clothes
Are clearly styled
Phones will capture
Their fake smiles
The filters make it best

On this bench rests
A troubled teen
Cut by words
So cruel and mean
Feels forgotten
And unseen
And burdened by these tests

On this bench rests

A pair with plans
Yet they're no longer
Holding hands
When he reveals
Just where they stand
He speaks and she protests

On this bench rests
A lady lost
Outdated map
Might well be tossed
Craves direction
At any cost
We'll wait for her request

On this bench rests
A mellowed man
Not quick to rise
I doubt he can
He clutches to
His latest scan
It might get worse, I've guessed

On this bench rests
A wallet whipped
From purse or pocket
Must have slipped
Then was emptied
Now it's stripped

Perhaps they'll reinvest

On this bench rests
A caring cause
Where thoughts can sing
Without applause
An opportunity
To pause
See what the bench suggests

14 Yellow Crayons

14 yellow crayons for my muse
And half of them were broken into twos
How could you expect
An average fellow
To create a masterpiece
In nothing but yellow

Of course, you have the obvious bright fruits
Like a pineapple upon a patterned suit
Rubber ducky chewing squash
Or a chick chewing cheese
Couldn't think of any others
Didn't want to draw these

Next I drew some daffodils in fields
Draped with blankets of banana peels
A giant vat of butter
A taxi filled with corn
My eyes were getting blurry
I was starting to mourn

Had to draw a lemon and a sun
I can't say that I found it very fun
The canary drove the school bus
For a raincoat made of eggs

At this point I'd had it
Give me color, I begged

No ketchup, yes, I only had the mustard
And nothing left for topping off the custard
Thought I found a 15th crayon
Then saw it was a fry
This is useless, I relented
Couldn't laugh, only cry

A world with only one hue is insane
The rainbow must accompany the rain
If you limit your palette
To the colors you know
Your world will be missing
That red orange yellow green blue indigo violet
glow

The Muffin Men

Do we know
The muffin men
And have we been
To Drury Lane

Have we felt
The oven's heat
That warms their feet
While they wait

Dare we read
Their recipe
Or let it be
Their secret kept

Some swear they know
The muffin men
They told me when
I asked them

Hard to say
If I tried
To come inside
What I'd see

But for now
I'll ask around
Until I've found
The way in

I want to know
The muffin men
Perhaps then
I could bake, too